RHYMECRAFT

Sussex

Edited By Donna Samworth

First published in Great Britain in 2018 by:

Young Writers

Young Writers
Remus House
Coltsfoot Drive
Peterborough
PE2 9BF
Telephone: 01733 890066
Website: www.youngwriters.co.uk

All Rights Reserved
Book Design by Ashley Janson
© Copyright Contributors 2017
SB ISBN 978-1-78896-055-7
Printed and bound in the UK by BookPrintingUK
Website: www.bookprintinguk.com
YB0343T

FOREWORD

Welcome Reader, to *Rhymecraft - Sussex*.

Among these pages you will find a whole host of poetic gems, built from the ground up by some wonderful young minds. Included are a variety of poetic styles, from amazing acrostics to creative cinquains, from dazzling diamantes to fascinating free verse.

Here at Young Writers our objective has always been to help children discover the joys of poetry and creative writing. Few things are more encouraging for the aspiring writer than seeing their own work in print. We are proud that our anthologies are able to give young authors this unique sense of confidence and pride in their abilities as well as letting their poetry reach new audiences.

The editing process was a tough but rewarding one that allowed us to gain an insight into the blooming creativity of today's primary school pupils. I hope you find as much enjoyment and inspiration in the following poetry as I have, so much so that you pick up a pen and get writing!

Donna Samworth

CONTENTS

Brede Primary School, Broad Oak

Madeline Pearce (8)	1
Kaya Masters (8)	2
Umar Ilham (10)	3
Lochie Barrington-Peek (8)	4
Jude Peters (9)	5
Madison Ives (8)	6
Clio Ansell (8)	7
Kiera McCarthy (8)	8
Martin Tunbridge (8)	9
James Harrison (8)	10
Louie Kelly (8)	11
Tyler Wren (8)	12

Castlewood Primary School, Southwater

Emma Ruth Butler (8)	13
Rayyan Ahmed (8)	14
Aliesha Emily Tyler (8)	15
Alanna Flynn (9)	16
Isabella Sophie Delo (9)	17
Jacob Brand (8)	18
Theo Thomas Botevyle (8)	19
Elise Hayward (8)	20
Esme Anstee-Brown (8)	21
Rachel Stringer (8)	22
Olivia Francis (8)	23
Caroline Brading (9)	24
Louis Coshan (8)	25
Neve Bills (9)	26
James Seaman (8)	27
Riley James Darkins (9)	28
Reuben Spikesman (8)	29
Leon Fatehnia (8)	30

Grace Killian (8)	31
Chloe Anne Watts (8)	32
Callum Lowe (8)	33

Central CE Academy, Chichester

Xander Nathaniel Lintag (10)	34
Alexander Darby (9)	36
Charlie Myall (9)	37
Noah Collins (9)	38
Emma Whitham (9)	40
Lewis Kemp (10)	41
Josh Kerr (9)	42
Rufus Strohacker (9)	43
Ella Louise Hill (9)	44
Toby Treagus (9)	45
Mercedes Clare Osborne (10)	46
Olivia Steele (9)	47
Jessica Dyson (9)	48
Taylor England (9)	49
Henry Court (9)	50
Logan Hunt (9)	51
George David Smith (9)	52
Alfie Brewer (9)	53
David Fischer (9)	54
Tilly Sparrow (9)	55
Hollie-Blossom Norris (9)	56
Lexiee-Lei Suzanne Jayne Turner (9)	57
Sam Wyatt (9)	58
Lily Clive (9)	59
Isabella Hill (9)	60
José Turner (9)	61
Finley (10)	62
Lily Luther (9)	63
Lily Mae Trinder (9)	64

Five Ashes CE Primary School, Five Ashes

Elysia Dear (10)	65
Charlotte Nickols (8)	66
Mavianne Munoz (10)	67
Claudia Pearson (8)	68
Rose Quintana (8)	69
Ellie Nickols (7)	70
Maisie Nash (7)	71
Ronnie Godfrey (8)	72
Amy Rebecca Packham (10)	73
Tom Vincent-Smith (8)	74
Roman Bitca (9)	75
Eviemarie Shepperson (10)	76
Poppy Neve (9)	77
Roman Henry Nash (8)	78

Maidenbower Junior School, Maidenbower

Brooke Diamond (9)	79
Donovan Patrick Reid (10)	80
Sophie Kaye (7)	82
Anwita Konduru (9)	83
Matilda Sumal (9)	84
Eva Grace Freestone (9)	85
Lakshita Jeyavelan (9)	86
Mia Cottee (8)	87
Sara Liaqat (10)	88
Holly Angelina Forbes-Whitear (10)	89
Beau George Richardson (9)	90
Tasia Nila Murdymootoo (7)	91
Calleigh Nicole Everett (8)	92
Jayden Hollens (8)	93
Clara Faye Hickmott (7)	94
Bronte Morphew (9)	95
Archie Ronnie Taylor (8)	96
Lewis Biggs (9)	97

Mark Cross CE Primary School, Mark Cross

Charlotte Caroline Elliott-Lloyd (10)	98

Peasmarsh CE Primary, Peasmarsh

Brandon Joe Thornton (9)	99
Mollee Anne Owen (11)	100

Shipley CE Primary School, Shipley

Alice Rose Eager (10)	101
Holly Kent (11)	102
Saffron Alys Farmer (10)	104
Josh Peacock (9)	105
Max Basey (9)	106
Laurie Atkinson (10)	107
Henry Timm, (11)	108
Connor Marks (9)	109
Harry Giles (10)	110

St Margaret's CE School, Rottingdean

Malena Clarke-Fogg (7)	111
Josh Gilbert (8)	112
Leonardo St Louis (7)	113
Ceri Williams (8)	114
Oscar James (8)	115
Bobby Harding (8)	116
Isabella Fisher Jones (7)	117
Daisy Waller (7)	118
Coco Bonnie Love Crane (7)	119
Isla Simson (8)	120
Kai Sanz Oliveira (7)	121

St Mary Star Of The Sea School, St Leonards-On-Sea

Christie Winthe (8)	122
Neill Cuison (8)	123
Connor Michael Ralph (9)	124
Scarlett Megazue Assignon (8)	125
Janine Ibao Dela Peña (7)	126
Sophia Collins (8)	127
Jack Gasson (8)	128
Kennedy Assetto (9)	129
Krisna Pun (8)	130
Jenson Jeneslas Jeyakumar (8)	131
Cansin Arya Can (8)	132

St Paul's CE Primary School & Nursery, Brighton

Ava Stephenson (7)	133
Amaya Paun (7)	134
Maddie Shotten (7)	135
Zhiyi Sun (7)	136
Elsa Cheung (7)	137
Gellért Tandary (8)	138

Upper Beeding Primary School, Upper Beeding

Tom Welstead (10)	139
Lara Vielvoye (10)	140
Poppy Johnson (10)	142
Nova Redman (10)	143
Layla Antunovich (9)	144
Josh Brian Munns (10)	145

THE POEMS

Seasons

The seasons come and seasons go.
Here comes summer, there goes summer.
It's hot a lot in summer.
The sun is here.
Some days are rainy but mostly it's sunny.

The seasons come and seasons go.
Here comes winter and here goes winter.
The snow is like a huge sheet of paper.
Some days it doesn't snow but mostly it does.

The seasons come and seasons go.
They are sprinting by.
Here comes a season, there goes a season.
Sometimes it's hot, sometimes it's rainy,
Sometimes it's snowy.
The sun is lava,
The snow is a sheet of paper.

Madeline Pearce (8)
Brede Primary School, Broad Oak

A Dream For One

The rain mane unicorn comes galloping in spring.
The world of magic and colour.
The rain mane unicorn is velvet soft.

Flower Shower hops around in the summertime
With all the baby animals.
The world with a ball of fire.
Flower Shower has a flower dress of colour.

The conker squirrel scurries around
Searching for nuts.
The fun-filled world of nature.
The conker squirrel is as fluffy as a puppy.

The ice mice slip and slide on the frozen lake.
The wonderful world of winter.
The ice mice are snakes slithering to the other side.

Kaya Masters (8)
Brede Primary School, Broad Oak

Seasons

The sun blazing like a ball of lightning,
With children having a lot of fun in the sun,
Seasons changing, what's your favourite?
Autumn's up next with leaves falling.
About to change into beautiful colours.
Like ambers, orange, rose-red
And crispy, crunchy glowing gold.
Animals hibernating, squirrels,
Badgers and hedgehogs.
Next is spring. As the Earth springs into action,
The animals are waking up.
The trees and plants
Are getting a lot of sunshine and water.

Umar Ilham (10)
Brede Primary School, Broad Oak

The Farm Animals

Pig, goose, cow, moose,
They live on a farm, in a barn.
On the farm it's very calm.

The farm doesn't get any calmer...
When the farmer buys an elephant!

All the animals sleeping
Until they hear a weeping.
It's the elephant,
Crying at a mouse!

Lochie Barrington-Peek (8)
Brede Primary School, Broad Oak

The Tiger

In a humid jungle I suddenly hear something.
I see a huge, furry tiger behind a bush.
His claws are like knives.
His roar is like a volcano erupting
And his teeth are as sharp as daggers.
His fur is as bright as the hot sun.
His prey is so delicious
Thanks to all his teeth!

Jude Peters (9)
Brede Primary School, Broad Oak

The Elegant Horse Dream

The soft white horse appeared
in my elegant dream.

The horse all alone
in the dark and creepy woods.

His mane flowing in the wind
like the long grass in the meadow.

His hooves are clippety-clopping
through the dull woods.

Madison Ives (8)
Brede Primary School, Broad Oak

Nocturnal Animals

It's turning into night, the animals are walking.
It's not very light, their beds are a-making.
The fox's tail is a fluffy blanket.
The leaves on the floor are like a carpet.
The animals are noisy like a tambourine.
Orange, handsome fox; tiny little bean.

Clio Ansell (8)
Brede Primary School, Broad Oak

Cats

The cat's fur is silky smooth
Like whipped cream.

Munching, crunching biscuits,
Snuggling gently, hear them purr.

A king of the bed!
Sprawling across the warm, comfy blankets.

Kiera McCarthy (8)
Brede Primary School, Broad Oak

Animals

My hamster is fluffier than a piece of cotton wool.
Dashing around on a roller coaster.
At night, feet whizzing like a duck's underwater.
Puffed-up cheeks stuffed with food.
Sprinting down the tube.

Martin Tunbridge (8)
Brede Primary School, Broad Oak

Minecraft

Zombie, zombie,
Don't get in his way.
Build yourself a base,
Don't be his prey!

Digging deep in a cave,
Mining in the night.
Keep a look out,
Husks are in sight!

James Harrison (8)
Brede Primary School, Broad Oak

The Beach In Summer

Sunny honey in the sky
The sun is fiery
Buzzing soldiers are working hard
Busy, bustling beaches
Splashing, swimming
The burning sand tickling toes.

Louie Kelly (8)
Brede Primary School, Broad Oak

The Beach

Waves *crash, bang, boom!*
The waves race to shore.
Stones crash around my feet.
Sand sparkles like glitter.
Baby-blue clouds fly across the sky.

Tyler Wren (8)
Brede Primary School, Broad Oak

Friendship Is Great!

F riendship is great
R ainy days are fun when your friends come around to splash and play
I love having friends, they are so much fun
E veryone is so nice when they are your friends
N ow I know friendship is great because friends are so kind
D on't fight with friends because then they won't be your friends
S o you should like your friends
H aving friends is great
I love having friends
P laying with friends is very enjoyable.

Emma Ruth Butler (8)
Castlewood Primary School, Southwater

Animal Adventure!

Orange parrots look like carrots.
Cheetahs blast like fast cars.
Giraffes are tall like a skyscraper.
Rabbits hop like a bouncy spring.
Elephants are so huge like a castle.
Lions roar like a person screams.
Wolves growl like a bear roars.
Tigers have claws as sharp as knives.
Rhinoceroses have horns that are like broken glass.
Owls howl like an animal's bark.
Frogs are sticky like glue.
Monkeys swing in the trees in the winter breeze.
Every animal has an ability!

Rayyan Ahmed (8)
Castlewood Primary School, Southwater

My Indonesian Life

Life in Indonesia is so hot,
I can always find a sweltering spot.

This place is so surprising,
When I come it'll be amazing!

I think the food here is really nice,
Because they add a hint of spice.

This place is so surprising,
When I come it'll be amazing!

Indonesia is such a surprise,
Especially the glamorous sunrise!

This place is so surprising,
When I come it'll be amazing!

Aliesha Emily Tyler (8)
Castlewood Primary School, Southwater

Walking By The Harbour

Walking by the harbour.
Listening to the night-time breeze.
Gazing at the twinkling stars above me.

It's beginning to get cold
And is starting to rain.
Fear gathers in my brain,
I run as fast as I can,
For lightning has just struck.
Hopefully tomorrow, I will have some luck.

Home is just around the corner,
Safe at last.
Snuggled up in the duvet,
Watching the storm go past.

Alanna Flynn (9)
Castlewood Primary School, Southwater

The Life Of Nature

Nature is something to explore,
It's as ferocious as before.
Full of wildlife, living in the trees,
As well as the buzzing bees.

Flowers and buds leisurely grow,
Lakes and rivers are extremely shallow.
Long swaying grass is more towering than ever,
The flying bird drops a feather.

Beautiful greenery will never come to an end,
This is the life of nature!

Isabella Sophie Delo (9)
Castlewood Primary School, Southwater

The Poem About Chelsea

C helsea are a good team, they play fast.
H elpful passes give them a chance to score.
E nd of first half, get a break.
L unch break, get a good snack and rest.
S ent to the pitch to play, winning 2-0.
E nd of match is in 20 minutes, we might win the cup.
A nd it's the end of the match. Everton lost and Chelsea won the cup and had a good celebration!

Jacob Brand (8)
Castlewood Primary School, Southwater

Brighton

B righton is my favourite team.
R ound the Premier League table they go.
I think Brighton will stay up.
G oing against teams that won't win the cup.
H igh up in the table means no relegation.
T hem staying up means they will have a celebration.
O n and on they go, playing like pros.
N ot at all wanting to doze.

Theo Thomas Botevyle (8)
Castlewood Primary School, Southwater

Halloween

H ats, cats, costumes and sweets
A llsorts, yummy for my tummy
L ollipops and pirates,
L iquorice too
O n Halloween people often say 'boo'
W itches are scary, so are those clowns
E ating those sweets make me go 'blahh'
E ek! Who is that?
N ever knowing who is lurking in the dark...

Elise Hayward (8)
Castlewood Primary School, Southwater

Sea Animals

S ea animals swim in groups.
E els slithering under your feet.
A dolphin jumps past every day.

A shark is lurking
N o fish are near.
I 'll bet jellyfish are bubbling by.
M anta rays flying by.
A turtle swims past.
L ying down on the ground.
S ea is a wonderful place.

Esme Anstee-Brown (8)
Castlewood Primary School, Southwater

Seasons Are Great!

S ummer is excellent because the flowers bloom.
E ventually winter comes, crispy and crunchy.
A utumn breeze in my face.
S pring is wonderful and exciting because the birds sing.
O h how lovely the seasons are.
N ow I know that winter is chilly and breezy.
S ummer is excellent because the flowers bloom.

Rachel Stringer (8)
Castlewood Primary School, Southwater

Animals

A mazing zebras running so fast.
N ight-stalking predators looking for their prey.
I see huge elephants with those big tusks.
M onkeys climbing up trees to get bananas.
A bility for parrots to be funny.
L ots of kids here to see the animals.
S leepy animals at the end of the day!

Olivia Francis (8)
Castlewood Primary School, Southwater

Nature Is A Wonderful Place

N ature is a place of adventure,
A plant is growing and a stream is flowing,
T rees with their leaves don't attract that many bees,
U p high, birds fly in the sky,
R ound the corner a flower is huge and its petals are blue,
E nter the garden, it's like an imaginary world!

Caroline Brading (9)
Castlewood Primary School, Southwater

Tottenham

T ottenham are amazing
O n and on, playing at Wembley
T o the pitch... let's win!
T hanks to Harry Kane
E ven Dele Alli can help
N ow Hugo can give us a yelp
H ow Spurs play with grace
A nd now they are ace
M eeting the net a lot.

Louis Coshan (8)
Castlewood Primary School, Southwater

Christmas

C oldness,
H ibernating animals,
R aining with snowflakes,
I n the chilly Christmas breeze.
S leigh bells ring,
T rees full of ice,
M y presents are so good!
A ltogether on Christmas Day,
S parkling lights, brighten up the night.

Neve Bills (9)
Castlewood Primary School, Southwater

Seasons

S easons mean changes,
E very autumn has leaves falling,
A t night, the moon makes light,
S pring brings newborn animals,
O n summer nights, it's not that dark,
N ever in winter will there not be Christmas,
S easons change four times a year!

James Seaman (8)
Castlewood Primary School, Southwater

Arsenal

A rsenal, they've got the ball
R escuing their team in the 89th minute
S o they're two up now
E xcellent win over Spurs
N ow Olivier Giroud is coming on
A rsenal are better than Chelsea
L ost against Liverpool but, oh well!

Riley James Darkins (9)
Castlewood Primary School, Southwater

Koala

K oalas crave cuddling humans.
O ften koalas snuggle each other.
A nd for every meal they have leaves.
L ove hugs, you'll adore them so much you'll want to have one, but you can't.
'A fter fun, it's time for dinner,' says Mummy Koala.

Reuben Spikesman (8)
Castlewood Primary School, Southwater

Untitled

Choosing teams.
Ref throws the ball up.
We start tackling.
Pass it to the striker.
He shoots.
Great save!
But he puts the rebound in.
Dab to celebrate.
The goalkeeper boots it up the pitch.
Amazing goal!
The whistle goes.
Same sides next play?

Leon Fatehnia (8)
Castlewood Primary School, Southwater

Horses

H appy horses play in the meadow while eating grass.
O ut and about they are.
R unning around all day while they graze.
S unny days are the absolute best.
E ating plants is what they like to do.
S uperb pets they are!

Grace Killian (8)
Castlewood Primary School, Southwater

Dream Land!

Drifting away,
Drifting to the fantasy world of Dream Land.
Dreaming of Cake Island,
Houses of cake,
Castles of cake
And dogs of cake!

Suddenly... you're awake,
Looking for your cake!
You realise... it was a dream!

Chloe Anne Watts (8)
Castlewood Primary School, Southwater

The Famous CFC

Chelsea are better than Everton.
Hazard is sub.
Costa is striker.
Courtois is goalie.
Chelsea are the best team.
Watching them live is a dream!

Callum Lowe (8)
Castlewood Primary School, Southwater

Animals And Monsters

Animals are as beautiful as the night,
And some of them are very bright.
Some of them are really small,
And some are just too dumb so they fall.
Let me introduce one of them,
Here's the basic clucky hen.

Cows are really good for food,
Please don't kill these cute creatures dude!
Some pigs are as pink as flowers,
They don't like water so they don't take showers.
Sheep are as fluffy as wool,
Don't eat them or you'll be cruel.
Animals are really cool
And a monster is just a big fool!

Zombies, skeletons and spiders are just evil,
Like the Devil.
Ender Dragon is the final boss,
And one time I named him Ross.

The Wither is as hard as a rock,
At least he doesn't stink like a dirty sock.
This is a poem about monsters and animals
And I'm really sad that there's no camels.

Xander Nathaniel Lintag (10)
Central CE Academy, Chichester

The Ghost Boy

There was a ghost boy,
His name was Jack,
He had a dog that was black.
When he went to say hello
People called him a marshmallow.

So he went back to his house,
All there was, was a dead mouse.
He was very lonely back there,
And all he was, was thin air.

Nobody liked him so he shouted in a sob,
'My only friend is the dog.'
After that day in the hay,
All he did was play.

They never saw him after that,
They didn't even see his bat.
There was a ghost, his name was Jack,
He's gone for now
But he's gonna come back.

Alexander Darby (9)
Central CE Academy, Chichester

Pet Cats

Cats are so small that they fit in a boot.
They are so scared, they won't go in a pool.
Cats are fluffy so they get hot,
They barely ever drink water from their pot.

Cats are good for a pet,
You don't need to trap them in a net.
Cats don't do anything to scare you,
They're not going to wake you up and say boo!

If you want a cat
Wave bye to rats.
No more seagulls chirping,
The lovely sound of cats purring.
They will always be asleep,
Until you call him for a treat.

Charlie Myall (9)
Central CE Academy, Chichester

My Monster, Blob

I've got a monster,
Whose name is Blob.
Feeding my monster
Is a great big job.

He cries,
He whines,
But then he's fine,
He slowly slithers all the time.

He's a slimy grimy,
Sloppy slug.
He likes eating cabbages,
With a big fat bug.

He lives in a lawnmower,
All through October.
He's big as a mouse,
Dirty as a louse.

He's as neat
As my grandmother's feet,

He's loud
As a roaring crowd.
Blob.

That is why he's my best friend!

Noah Collins (9)
Central CE Academy, Chichester

The Sleek Snow Leopard

In the glittering snow
My paws barely show.
My pads are getting sore
So now I'm not quite sure.
Should I keep on going?
Because now my fears are showing.
As I reach the top, the Northern Lights are glowing.
My dappled fur is damp
So I think I need to make a camp.
I found a jagged cave.
It looks kind of like a grave.
As I'm at the top
Sitting next to a rock
I think my journey's come to an end
But I still haven't found a friend.

Emma Whitham (9)
Central CE Academy, Chichester

Minecraft Terrorists

Creepers, zombies, skeletons and spiders
Endermen, Ender Dragon, scuttlers and gardens.
All part of the Minecraft hell.
Some at a different level.
Steve and Alex looking for diamonds
But if they dig below their feet
They're going to meet a fiery end.
If you mine the cobblestone
You will meet a silvery last bend.
When you find a dragon, be prepared
Because you might find
An undead creature lurking,
But what is hiding there?

Lewis Kemp (10)
Central CE Academy, Chichester

Star Wars

A battle so gigantic
It raged across the galaxy.
The rebels fought the empire,
Lightning-fast laser bullets
Flying through the air.
Stormtroopers trampling through
The worlds of aliens.
Rebel transporters trying to escape
From the empire's grasp.
The rebels are outnumbered
But they never give up.
The rebels wear a lot of leather.
Stormtroopers are the most powerful things.
Imperials devour everything.

Josh Kerr (9)
Central CE Academy, Chichester

The Cat

There is a cat
In a house,
That loves to eat a mouse.

The cat is very good at playing
Which is very funny,
He's just like his mummy.

He's very strong,
Just like King Kong.

But mischievous and brave,
He also likes to sunbathe.

He's cute with a white stripe
But also likes a fight.

Rufus Strohacker (9)
Central CE Academy, Chichester

Silly Dog

I found a dog
And his name is Paul
He's very, very small.

He's always cool
He wants me to always throw his ball.

He always barks
Because he loves the dark.

He saw a bean
And it was clean
He was super keen
To eat the bean.

The dog was ill
And I had to pay a bill.

Ella Louise Hill (9)
Central CE Academy, Chichester

Snakes

These mysterious creatures are called snakes,
They like to slither over rakes.

Some can glide,
Some like to slide.

Some swallow eggs,
They have no legs.

Some have bad bites,
Some have legendary fights.

Some snakes are vicious
But they don't taste delicious.

Toby Treagus (9)
Central CE Academy, Chichester

Music And Bands

I am loud,
I can shout.

I am loud,
People bowed.

When I leap,
They don't sleep.

When they sing
I am king.

The band is as loud as a lion, *roar!*
But when I stop, they want some more.

I always shout,
When my fans are about.

Mercedes Clare Osborne (10)
Central CE Academy, Chichester

Family

F amilies love and families hate.
A mazing friends help you through hard times.
M arvellous dads play with you all day.
I ncredible godparents checking on you from time to time.
L aughing with your siblings, having fun all day.
Y oung second cousins you carry around all day.

Olivia Steele (9)
Central CE Academy, Chichester

North Pole

N is for numb fingers
O is for ocean water
R is for rapid river
T is for too cold
H is for hearing the wind

P is for polar bears
O is for overcoming the cold
L is for Lapland
E is for expedition.

Jessica Dyson (9)
Central CE Academy, Chichester

Fishing

F loats go down
I magine you were in town
S haky rod when I get a fish
H ave lots of fish on my dish
I mpressed when I caught carp
N ight fishing in the dark
G ood catch today!

Taylor England (9)
Central CE Academy, Chichester

Football Match
(A kennings poem)

Rain pouring,
Crowd roaring,
Flamethrower flaming,
Hand shaking,
Whistle blowing,
Ball kicking,
Goal scoring,
Bad tackling,
Injury making,
Commentator howling,
Players winning,
Trophy lifting.

Henry Court (9)
Central CE Academy, Chichester

Football

F all over
O wn goal
O verhead kick
T eam spirit
B all goes in the back of the net
A mazing sport
L ong shot on goal
L ike to play left wing.

Logan Hunt (9)
Central CE Academy, Chichester

Alien

A is for advanced technology.
L is for long-lost life of aliens since dinosaurs.
I is for intelligent knowledge.
E is for Ender weapons.
N is for new technology made.

George David Smith (9)
Central CE Academy, Chichester

Space

S pace is awesome
P arachutes come out of the capsule
A pollo 11 has now landed
C apsule is what astronauts land in
E xercise on the International Space Station.

Alfie Brewer (9)
Central CE Academy, Chichester

Space

S pace, the universe in the sky
P lanets in the solar system
A stronauts fly in rockets
C limbing into the shuttle
E agle has landed.

David Fischer (9)
Central CE Academy, Chichester

Apples

A pple crunch.
P ear punch.
P ears for the bears.
L aughing and eating apples in all kinds of weather.
E ating apples altogether.

Tilly Sparrow (9)
Central CE Academy, Chichester

Gymnastics

(A diamante poem)

Gymnastics
Amazing, hard work
Competitive, painful, strong
Gym family, workout, fun, flexible
Sweaty, gymnasts, joyful
Sore, conditioning
Skills.

Hollie-Blossom Norris (9)
Central CE Academy, Chichester

Space

S tars shining bright
P ieces of space that are so tight
A stronauts flying
C omet gliding past
E xperiencing space is great!

Lexiee-Lei Suzanne Jayne Turner (9)
Central CE Academy, Chichester

Zombie
(A kennings poem)

Day-ender
Fear-striker
Brain-sucker
Skull-cracker
Blood-drainer
Heart-ripper
Neck-chopper
Life-taker
Human-devourer
God-gobbler.

Sam Wyatt (9)
Central CE Academy, Chichester

Gymnastics

(A diamante poem)

Gymnastics
Hard, joyful
Amazing, happy, fun
Hot, steaming, competitive, strong
Flexible, family, sweaty
Achy, pain
Conditioning.

Lily Clive (9)
Central CE Academy, Chichester

Space

S mall planets.
P lanets moving.
A lways going round the sun.
C rashing into the moon.
E mpty void of space.

Isabella Hill (9)
Central CE Academy, Chichester

Earth! Sun!

(A diamante poem)

Sun
Bright, hot
Satisfying, red, light
Flickers, yellow, colourful, dark
Land, people, homes
Cars, life
Earth!

José Turner (9)
Central CE Academy, Chichester

Football

F ootball
O ver
O ffside
T ea
B reak
A ttack
L ow
L eap.

Finley (10)
Central CE Academy, Chichester

The Dog
(A diamante poem)

Dog
Love, rust
Hope, lost, family
Mad, lonely, small, sad
Barking, growing up, pretty
Brown, power
Special.

Lily Luther (9)
Central CE Academy, Chichester

Cats Vs Dogs

(A diamante poem)

Cats
Sleek, sly
Happy, soft, sleepy
Neat, proud, cute, fluffy
Friendly, excited, bouncy
Funny, crazy
Dogs.

Lily Mae Trinder (9)
Central CE Academy, Chichester

My Bubble World Of Dreams!

One night I was snuggled up under my house roof,
Then, all of a sudden, my dreams were set loose.
I thought I was half asleep,
But I was actually half awake!
My friend and I tread softly,
Such gentle steps we take
On big pillows of marshmallows.
Past our families we mouth our 'hellos'
Then we see our favourite pizza,
Wow, it's as big as the moon!
And then the biggest, best ice cream,
Complete with a giant spoon!
We play on bicycles made of bricks,
Make cakes from magic tricks.
What a day! What a night!
But really I'm lying down, snuggled tight.
Dreams are fun,
I wonder when I'll have the next one?

Elysia Dear (10)
Five Ashes CE Primary School, Five Ashes

The Seasons

The spring babies are hopping and skipping along fields of dandelions.
Munching on grass and sleeping in their cosy dens.
The summer sun is shining.
The flowers are blooming and the birds are singing sweet songs.
The autumn leaves are fireworks bursting in the wavy trees.
The green grass turns into white snow.
The snowflakes eat the leaves off the trees.
Animals hide in their warm, cosy burrows.

What lovely seasons!

Charlotte Nickols (8)
Five Ashes CE Primary School, Five Ashes

Popping Candy

Popping candy is so fun,
It pops in your mouth every second,
The unique taste for everyone,
The variety of flavours,
Jumping up and down in your mouth,
Like a box of frogs!
It's such a good party favour,
The noise they make is like barking dogs,
The shiny coating on them sparkles like the sun,
The joke on the packet is such a good pun,
I love them as a treat,
They make such a good sweet.

Mavianne Munoz (10)
Five Ashes CE Primary School, Five Ashes

Harvest Everywhere

Harvest is a time for sharing,
Harvest is a time for caring.
We all put on our welly boots,
To gather up the autumn fruit.

Crunchy carrots and crispy corn,
Autumn season has been born.
Orange pumpkins like the sun,
Getting ready for some Halloween fun!

Orange, brown, yellow and red,
Warm soup and yummy baked bread.
Harvest, harvest everywhere,
Harvest is a time to share.

Claudia Pearson (8)
Five Ashes CE Primary School, Five Ashes

Christmas Is Fun For Everyone!

C arol singing in the church,
H olly in an Advent ring.
R eindeer come on Christmas night,
I cy bells ring round their necks.
S now falling as family gather,
T urkey, large for all to eat.
M ince pies all hot and delicious,
A ngels smiling upon the tree.
S anta's coat, as red as a fire!

That's Christmas best for me!

Rose Quintana (8)
Five Ashes CE Primary School, Five Ashes

Firework

F izzing, whizzing, popping fireworks.
I lluminating glow sticks to light up the night.
R ed, orange, yellow, green, all the colours that can be.
E xploding, *bang, bang, bang!*
W ow, what a wonderful sight.
O h yum, look at those toffee apples.
R afe, Lottie, Daddy, Mummy, all go, 'Wow!'
K eep safe on Bonfire Night.

Ellie Nickols (7)
Five Ashes CE Primary School, Five Ashes

Friendship

In the spring friendship is beautiful.
In the spring fun can make your face bloom.
In summer friendship is great.
In summer fun is wonderful.
In autumn friendship is perfect.
In autumn fun is colourful.
In winter friendship is fun.
In winter fun is a warming heart.
Friendship and fun are great in the seasons
And I hope you agree.

Maisie Nash (7)
Five Ashes CE Primary School, Five Ashes

Shelby

The happiest face
The biggest green eyes
Shelby is my friend
He tells me no lies.

He always keeps me company
Especially when I'm sad
Shelby is my friend
Even when I'm bad.

He's been with me forever
We'll never be apart
Shelby is my friend
I love him with all my heart.

Ronnie Godfrey (8)
Five Ashes CE Primary School, Five Ashes

Big Dream

B ig day was coming up.
I t was the day where I get my pup!
G o straight to school.

D o swimming in the pool.
R un two miles.
E xtra big smiles
A nd meet my new best friend.
M y life was good but now it is fab!

Amy Rebecca Packham (10)
Five Ashes CE Primary School, Five Ashes

My Own Set Of Tools

Working with my daddy is so much fun,
He teaches me to measure
And we eat iced buns.

I drink tea from his flask
And he takes me to the café.

He lets me hammer in nails
And build little walls
But all I want is my own set of tools.

Tom Vincent-Smith (8)
Five Ashes CE Primary School, Five Ashes

In The Village

In the village I was born,
Were so many friends around.
We had many toys to play with,
In our little ground.

Helicopters, cars and Lego,
Little dollies for the girls.
We liked walking through the flowers,
We loved animals and birds.

Roman Bitca (9)
Five Ashes CE Primary School, Five Ashes

Friends Forever

You and me forever will be friends,
I'll help you out, any time.
Our friendship will always shine,
You're always there for me,
Your friendship sets me free
From all my sadness.
You and me forever will be friends.

Eviemarie Shepperson (10)
Five Ashes CE Primary School, Five Ashes

My House Poem

My house is tall, not small.
It has a wall, that's all.
It's bleak, not neat.
It's a freak, not chic.
It's weak, it has a leak,
I have only been there a week.

Poppy Neve (9)
Five Ashes CE Primary School, Five Ashes

Sun And Moon

(A diamante poem)

Sun
Warm, yellow
Blinding, burning, scorching
Fire, gas, rocks, core
Shining, changing, orbiting
Cold, white
Moon.

Roman Henry Nash (8)
Five Ashes CE Primary School, Five Ashes

Mobs, Mobs

Creepers in the night, screaming with fright.
Gotta hold onto my sword tight.
Risk it for a biscuit, should probably just skip it.
Now I'm sprinting back, my grip very slack.
Hid inside a cupboard with my three brothers.
When I fell out, I hit my head and said, 'Ouch!'
Zombies spawning, was excited for the morning.
Next day, ready to fight,
Hopefully I'm back before night.
Got my sword out of my chest,
Was a little bit scared have to confess.
Endermen spawning left to right,
As my diamond sword shone in the light.
Killing and slaying was the greatest feeling,
Crying with laughter while kneeling.

Brooke Diamond (9)
Maidenbower Junior School, Maidenbower

Technology

Phones being used,
Kids playing virtual games,
Electricity produced
Every single day.

Letters out the window,
Board games in the past,
People look on super screens
Until they will exhaust.

Money flying round,
Wires on the ground,
Nobody knows what is happening,
Everywhere is loud.

People trying to reach out,
Letters with no replies,
We're all using Cloud,
Nobody goes outside.

Happiness commencing,
Letters now arrive,
We can't depend on technology,
When we all have lives.

Donovan Patrick Reid (10)
Maidenbower Junior School, Maidenbower

My Cute Kitten

My cute kitten is called Kitty
But she never does knitting.

Kitty eats a whole tin of fish,
In a massive dish.

She goes through her cat flap
And comes in for a nap on my lap.

She chases some dogs,
But she's not a YouTuber
So she can't do blogs.

She gets fluff everywhere,
On the sofa and on the chair.

She's never gonna be fat
Because she doesn't eat anything black.

Sophie Kaye (7)
Maidenbower Junior School, Maidenbower

Rainbow

I am a very colourful thing and have seven colours.
Red, orange, yellow, green, blue, purple and pink.
You cannot reach me.
People like to see me and I am up in the sky.
You can only see me when it rains
but when it's also sunny at the same time.
I also form when the sun rays strike the raindrops
falling from the faraway rain cloud
and also opposite side of the sun.
I am a crescent shape.
What am I?

Anwita Konduru (9)
Maidenbower Junior School, Maidenbower

Midnight Fear

In the night,
Nobody knows what lurks about.
You'll be scared without a doubt,
Zombie thinks you're all mine
But don't get too close to the swamp
Or you will be squished by slime!

Don't look at an Enderman,
They are like Slenderman!

Well, now you know midnight is scary,
That's why there is such a thing as midnight fear.

Matilda Sumal (9)
Maidenbower Junior School, Maidenbower

Winter

Winter begins with Bonfire Night,
There is a chill in the air
And the leaves are all gone.
We look forward to December
Because Christmas won't be long,
The days have gone short
And the nights have gone dark.
Jack Frost is in the air
And he will bring a spark.
If it snows we will play,
Before a hot chocolate and a movie to end the day.

Eva Grace Freestone (9)
Maidenbower Junior School, Maidenbower

City Sounds Heard After Dark

Quiet songs from the empty bars.
Old drums banging near and far.

Aircraft zooming through the dark sky.
Rooftop cats that spit and cry.

Motorbikes with a sudden roar.
Noisy lads who slam the door.

The greedy dogs that growl and bark.
Whispers from the padlocked park.

City sounds heard after dark.

Lakshita Jeyavelan (9)
Maidenbower Junior School, Maidenbower

Leaves Are On The Go

Leaves fall on my knees.
I can see the wind knock leaves off trees.
People are kicking piles of yellow, red and orange leaves.
Conkers are round with spiky shells.
The snow knocks the berries off the holly.
The trees aren't gold because it's cold.
It looks like the trees have had a sneeze and lost all their leaves.

Mia Cottee (8)
Maidenbower Junior School, Maidenbower

Summer Dreams

Summer dreams
Are about having hope,
Trying to play outside,
Hearing the birds singing.
I hope I can get a ride,
The flowers are blossoming,
Try to have some dreams,
Dreams about dancing,
Having dreams about summer.
Have you ever had a summer dream?
I bet your friends have!
I hope you have a summer dream!

Sara Liaqat (10)
Maidenbower Junior School, Maidenbower

Building Blocks That Build My Home

Building blocks that build my home.
They keep me warm when winter comes.
Some winter days I get my blankie,
Cuddle up and look at the blocks.
My home is colourful,
My home is cute.
This is something you cannot dispute.
Building blocks that build my home,
My family live here, I'm never alone.

Holly Angelina Forbes-Whitear (10)
Maidenbower Junior School, Maidenbower

My Dog Slinky

He's long and strong
And he eats out of a bowl.

He's black and brown
And acts like a clown.

He's fun, fun, fun
And likes to run, run, run!

Sleeping is the thing he loves.
We always like to give him hugs.

Beau George Richardson (9)
Maidenbower Junior School, Maidenbower

The Funny Smiggle

Smiggle wiggles in the morning.
Smiggle niggles the parents.
Smiggle jiggles in the fridge.
Smiggle squiggles in the afternoon.
Smiggle wriggles the pens and pencils.
Smiggle giggles in the night.

Tasia Nila Murdymootoo (7)
Maidenbower Junior School, Maidenbower

Autumn

Longer nights will soon be here
Once the day has passed
Chilly winds shake the leaves to the ground
The light grey squirrel collects his nuts for winter
Crunchy leaves denote the frost
Summertime is finally lost

Calleigh Nicole Everett (8)
Maidenbower Junior School, Maidenbower

Saturn

S ixth planet from the sun
A gas giant
T hird largest planet
U ranus has rings too
R ings around it are yellow and gold
N ow spins faster than any other planet.

Jayden Hollens (8)
Maidenbower Junior School, Maidenbower

Bluebells In The Night

Bluebells are glistening bright
In the darkness of the night
Glistening thanks to the street lights
People pass and feel just right.
The wonder of nature glows
Even in the fading light.

Clara Faye Hickmott (7)
Maidenbower Junior School, Maidenbower

Butterfly

White, white clouds in the sky.
I look up to a butterfly.
All the white clouds in the sky
Covered up the butterfly.
Now it's time to say goodbye
To the pretty butterfly.

Bronte Morphew (9)
Maidenbower Junior School, Maidenbower

A Spider Called Meg

There once was a spider called Meg
Who broke off one of her legs
She hopped when she ran
Scared the life outta my nan
And never came back again.

Archie Ronnie Taylor (8)
Maidenbower Junior School, Maidenbower

Jaguar

J aw snapping
A ngry cat
G ood tree climber
U ndercover spy
A nimal eating
R iver swimming.

Lewis Biggs (9)
Maidenbower Junior School, Maidenbower

Life

Life is special,
You should treasure it like golden sand,
Shimmering underwater with crystals.

Life is given and taken,
Like a seed being planted, like a flower dying.
Always look closer into what seems distorted
But is actually beautiful.
Life is a key, a key to anything possible;
It can lead you on glorious journeys.
You will receive good things from good people
If you do good deeds.
Life is a gemstone... ruby, peridot, aquamarine,
Citrus, diamond, amethyst, sunstone,
Tourmaline and sapphire...

Everything this life gives us is incredible...
Live life and treasure it.

Life is great!

Charlotte Caroline Elliott-Lloyd (10)
Mark Cross CE Primary School, Mark Cross

Poem Craft

Mining, mining with my iron pick.
Trying to find diamonds, that's the trick!
Oh no, creeper! Run away quick!
If he catches up to me, he will make me sick!

Time is ticking, it's time to go,
Up to the surface, let's not go slow.
On the desert plains, trying to find home,
Luckily it's daylight,
Crossing the water, full of foam.

I am home.
Bedtime.
Zzzzz!

Brandon Joe Thornton (9)
Peasmarsh CE Primary, Peasmarsh

My Life Gone

Mining, mining in the dark,
I see morning light.
Quick, run!
Finally out of my mine...
It starts to darken,
Evening is on the horizon,
Run, run, before it's too late!
I see a creeper up ahead,
Oh no!
I bang into the mob and, *boom!*
That's my life gone.

Mollee Anne Owen (11)
Peasmarsh CE Primary, Peasmarsh

How Not To Be Loved

I was too big to be loved - to be hugged,
They all looked away,
Then I got the shove,
They pushed me off Atlantic,
And that's when I said,
I'm free - but lost inside.

I saw Titanic gleaming with love,
They were all laughing and thought nothing happened,
At the time, I knew they were going to die - at least some,
I know I shouldn't have done it... I know,
You should have seen them - that's why I did her tip,
No one forgave me - I just melted away,
'Till I was as small as an ice cube.
I looked back... what have I done?

Alice Rose Eager (10)
Shipley CE Primary School, Shipley

The Night Of Horror

Three years I waited,
Then I set off on my journey,
I went to Southampton and picked up those who desired me.

Then it came to the last day of my life,
On the 14th of April, what a bad day,
Late at night a sharp-looking iceberg struck me.

I know I was heading for a watery death,
They led me into fog without a thought,
The greedy first-class passengers went first saying;
'My dress!'

Third class were last,
I thought they should have gone first,
It was the 15th of April - I thought it would end like this.

Men didn't leave the Titanic,
Some women stayed with their loved ones,
People scurried to the lifeboats.

Now I lay in my death place,
Under the evil monster sea,
Think of the one I regret hitting.

Holly Kent (11)
Shipley CE Primary School, Shipley

Last Light

There was a big boat, a big boat it was,
It sank in the middle of the night because...
They sailed far away in the icy sea,
And crashed into an iceberg while having their tea!
The captain heard and although he did care,
Titanic sank with no room to spare,
Some people rowed away, they rowed for their lives,
It was ladies first, children and wives,
Some stayed in their cabin so they could die together,
This tragic story will last forever.
I wonder...
Would I be a lucky survivor that night?
Or, would I stay on board and witness my last light?

Saffron Alys Farmer (10)
Shipley CE Primary School, Shipley

The Titanic

Titanic was coming, she was going to crash,
She was going to thump, wallop and bash.
People started handing out life jackets, saying,
'You first, not me.'
Everyone in the café got up and threw away their tea.
All the people in the boiler room scurried for their lives.
Passengers ran, even husbands and wives.
Children and mums and men with their friends.
So remember this tragic day when it all ends...

Josh Peacock (9)
Shipley CE Primary School, Shipley

Terrific Titanic's Terrible Grave

I'm sitting down in the Titanic.
I've travelled long and far,
Holding onto a bar.
This mighty sea,
Brushing against me.
Then we hit a block of ice,
We hit it, it wasn't nice!
14th April 1912 was a tragic day.

This amazing boat!
The fog made it worse.
This boat was meant to be unsinkable,
But now it's just unthinkable.
It was sinking, sinking down to its grave,
This night I, Max and Dad died.

Max Basey (9)
Shipley CE Primary School, Shipley

Pokémon Madness

Oh hi, I'm Pikachu.
I'm a Pokémon, who are you?
Oh no, here they come.
Trainers, trainers, run, run, run!
Look over there a Cubchoo
Ha, ha, ha, I caught you.
Hey look a Steelix.
Shouted little Felix.
They found and caught.
Oh goodness what a sport.
Then they're left with me...
Suddenly they said:
'Would you like some tea?'

Laurie Atkinson (10)
Shipley CE Primary School, Shipley

Last Words

I was there at that very moment
Travelling through the sea
At the speed of no other ship
No one could see me

My last sail and dip
To the place of New York, I'll see
To the shore I'll be...

There I was, sinking down to the ocean's depth
Where I felt the water shiver on
That was the day I sank
April 15th, 1912.

Henry Timm, (11)
Shipley CE Primary School, Shipley

Titanic's Death

A ship's mighty glory, falling to the sea
I wish I could do more to set the people free.
The stupidness of 1st class
Risking their lives for clothes
That disastrous day I can never forget it.
All those lives lost to a grave
Of hard steel and stone.

Connor Marks (9)
Shipley CE Primary School, Shipley

Titanic's Torn Tongue

My death was very devastating,
Like the shattering of the seas,
But my life did not end there...
I built a life of regret
I died in the boiler room
I didn't make it in time
And I suffocated to death
With some haunted treasure inside.

Harry Giles (10)
Shipley CE Primary School, Shipley

Yesterday

Y esterday it rained
E very single second.
S tuck inside all day.
T o do doodles in my book.
E very minute was boring.
R aincoats and wellies, I put them on.
D ived outside and jumped in puddles
A nd finally it stopped.
Y esterday it rained.

Malena Clarke-Fogg (7)
St Margaret's CE School, Rottingdean

Untitled

Fire burning in the night
Flaming heat all over the room
Add some more wood
And it flashes like lightning.
Once the fire is out
The smell of burning still remains.
Now you're warm,
Nice and cosy
It's time to go to bed.

Josh Gilbert (8)
St Margaret's CE School, Rottingdean

Dolphins

In the ocean of dreams
There were five glittering dolphins
Playing in the rain.

Whales came to scare them
With a heavy duty crane.

Penguins, crocodiles and sharks came
And saved the dolphins from the crane.

Leonardo St Louis (7)
St Margaret's CE School, Rottingdean

Minecraft Build Up!

Build in light,
Never in dark...
Unless you want to die!
A day's ten minutes
And so is night.
Beware of things at night
Because they will fright!
Get yourself an ocelot
To get away from creepers!

Ceri Williams (8)
St Margaret's CE School, Rottingdean

Explosions + Fire = TNT!

Experiment with it on your friend's houses
Or make a trap out of its deadly powers.
TNT is the block of war.
If you have it in a Hunger Game
You'll be invincible.

Oscar James (8)
St Margaret's CE School, Rottingdean

Best Free Kick In The World

On the pitch
I got a free kick.
The ball hit
The back of the net.
The crowd went wild.
My teammates cheered
And knocked me to the ground!

Bobby Harding (8)
St Margaret's CE School, Rottingdean

Yummy, Yummy Food
(Haiku poetry)

I am hungry now.
Any deliveries sent.
Yes, food to eat now.

I've eaten it now.
It was very yummy food.
I enjoyed the food.

Isabella Fisher Jones (7)
St Margaret's CE School, Rottingdean

The Lost Bear

Once I saw a polar bear
But it jumped onto an ice cube.
It sailed away
But two days later it came back
And everyone was so happy.

Daisy Waller (7)
St Margaret's CE School, Rottingdean

The Witch

A witch lived in her cottage.
She was nice, with a black cat.
The witch would make nice potions
But the cat would just hunt mice!

Coco Bonnie Love Crane (7)
St Margaret's CE School, Rottingdean

Unicorn Magic

In the dream of the magic land
I found a pink and purple unicorn,
It had a glistening mane blowing in the wind!

Isla Simson (8)
St Margaret's CE School, Rottingdean

Wolf Eye

(A haiku poem)

Teeth as sharp as knives
Nocturnal throughout the night
Eyes as bright as light.

Kai Sanz Oliveira (7)
St Margaret's CE School, Rottingdean

Freedom Is...

Freedom is being yourself,
Tomboy or girly,
Whatever you like.
Freedom is being free from slavery,
Yes, I mean it,
Quit being a slave.
Freedom is having fun,
With no fear of what your race is.
Freedom is expressing your feelings,
Cry and shout or dance about.
Freedom is releasing your worries,
Of course
They too are free from there.
Freedom is allowing others to be free too,
Sure,
They can be what they want.
Freedom means different things to different people,
But what does it mean to you?

Christie Winthe (8)
St Mary Star Of The Sea School, St Leonards-On-Sea

Freedom

Enjoy the freedom that you have,
Fly free,
Everything you dream of is what you'll get,
Release yourself.

Let the bird out of the cage!

Believe in your own beliefs,
Express your feelings,
Find who you are,
Never give up!

Let the bird out of the cage!

He glides like an angel,
He is the light to his family,
He's the rider to a horse,
He wants his freedom.

The bird is free!

Neill Cuison (8)
St Mary Star Of The Sea School, St Leonards-On-Sea

Freedom

F reedom is where you get a chance to find out who you are.
R un wild doing what you want to do.
E xpress your emotions and feelings.
E scape the indoors and play with your friends, doing what you want.
D o what you feel like doing wherever and whenever you want.
O pen the doors and go outside.
M ake yourself a better person.

Connor Michael Ralph (9)
St Mary Star Of The Sea School, St Leonards-On-Sea

Freedom

Freedom, like a bird flies.
Freedom, not stressed like I used to be.
Freedom, when you can smell fresh air.
Hmm, I smell fresh air.
Freedom, I love it.
Freedom, playing with friends.

Freedom.
Freedom.
Freedom...

Now I feel relaxed.
Now I feel free.
Now I will be all that I can be.

Scarlett Megazue Assignon (8)
St Mary Star Of The Sea School, St Leonards-On-Sea

Freedom

F reedom is a gift to everyone
R elease your feelings
E rase your worries and think positive
E xpress the gift of freedom
D o what's right for yourself
O nly you can choose what to do
M ake people choose what they want to be in life, not to be forced by others.

Janine Ibao Dela Peña (7)
St Mary Star Of The Sea School, St Leonards-On-Sea

Freedom Poem

Freedom is having fun and being yourself and by yourself.
Release people who want to be free all by themselves.
Express your feelings when someone wants to be free.
Don't push somebody when you want to have freedom.
Often people run when they want freedom.
Make yourself a better person.

Sophia Collins (8)
St Mary Star Of The Sea School, St Leonards-On-Sea

Freedom To All

F reedom takes you further
R elease your body
E xpress your feelings
E very day, people get to do what they want
D o what you want
O ur opinions are the best
M eet your friends.

Freedom to all!

Jack Gasson (8)
St Mary Star Of The Sea School, St Leonards-On-Sea

Freedom

Gently,
The enclosed seed
Is put in the ground.

Scared,
The seed sees flowing water coming,
The seed goes damp.

Many days have passed,
The seed is now a tree,
It is beautiful,
It is wonderful,
It is free.

Kennedy Assetto (9)
St Mary Star Of The Sea School, St Leonards-On-Sea

Freedom!

Freedom!
It is a gift.
But others are trapped.
Others don't have freedom.
Others are kicked out of their homes.

But no matter what...

Be your only boss!
No one bosses you!
Everyone has the right to be free!

Krisna Pun (8)
St Mary Star Of The Sea School, St Leonards-On-Sea

Freedom

F ight for freedom
R un to freedom
E veryone deserves freedom
E veryone has a right to be free
D o what you want to do
O nly you can be who you want to be
M andela was free.

Jenson Jeneslas Jeyakumar (8)
St Mary Star Of The Sea School, St Leonards-On-Sea

Freedom

Freedom is having fun.
Freedom is being able to speak in front of people.
Freedom is escaping.
Freedom is being safe.
Freedom is fighting danger.
Freedom is sitting at home.
Freedom is making people happy.

Cansin Arya Can (8)
St Mary Star Of The Sea School, St Leonards-On-Sea

Animals In The Zoo

There's big grey elephants and kangaroos
And long-beaked pelicans in the zoo.
Rabbits are fluffy and white,
Very snowy alright.
Guinea pigs are fun but shy,
Monkeys like eating banana pie.
Parrots are colours of the rainbow,
They always say hello.
Tigers are orange and stripy,
Hippos are fat and mighty.
Crocodiles are green and snappy
And seals are really clappy.

There hang sloths and bats
And gorillas stealing hats.
Giraffes are tall,
Lions are loud
And jaguars are really cool.

Ava Stephenson (7)
St Paul's CE Primary School & Nursery, Brighton

Baking

I had a dream the other day...
I ate whipped cream.
My friend baked a cake,
She said it was fun to make.
The vanilla creamy cake.
I tasted, it was fake!
Mixed up with chocolate chips,
I couldn't even cut it.
It looked very wild
But it was very mild.
It's very hot.
Can you see the chocolate dots?
I make my cookies up,
I hope they give you luck.
Mix the dough all up,
Then clean up all your muck.
Colouring blue, colouring new,
Which one's best for you?

Amaya Paun (7)
St Paul's CE Primary School & Nursery, Brighton

Water

I really, really like the sea
And all my friends come and play with me.
When I am out, I play about.
I really, really like to swim,
Especially when I jump in.
It is brilliant, salty and cold as well
But swimming pools are cosy and warm as well.
Seas are stormy, pools are splashy.

Maddie Shotten (7)
St Paul's CE Primary School & Nursery, Brighton

Friends

I'm really kind
But I really don't mind
And I really like playing with my friends.
When they play with me, it's fun
But I'm always on a run.
I am joyful
But I am not helpful.
I am happy
And I am not mean.

Zhiyi Sun (7)
St Paul's CE Primary School & Nursery, Brighton

Animal Poem

Camels are mammals.
Zebras are stripy.
The monkeys are in a hurry.
They are very furry.
The elephants are starting to stampede right now!
The hippos are swimming round and round.

Elsa Cheung (7)
St Paul's CE Primary School & Nursery, Brighton

Dogs

I like dogs because they are fun
They really like to run in the sun
They really like to sleep
And go to the kitchen
For something to eat.

Gellért Tandary (8)
St Paul's CE Primary School & Nursery, Brighton

Off To The Swimming Pool I Go!

It is dark and cold, early one day,
Time to wake up, I hear Mummy say.
We're up before everyone to go to the pool,
Quite frankly, I think it's better than school!
I pull on my trunks and my swimming hat,
Also my goggles, shaped like the eyes of a cat.
I walk down the steps, nice and slow,
I push off from the wall and off I go!
Two lengths of breaststroke and two on my back,
Then front crawl for two, while my muscles crack.
Do it again and again until I'm puffed,
Can't wait to get home and eat till I'm stuffed!
I really love swimming
And I've become pretty good,
I'll keep practising until I swim like I should.
Perhaps one day I'll swim as a pro,
But for now I'm happy giving it a go!

Tom Welstead (10)
Upper Beeding Primary School, Upper Beeding

Birds

A robin, my robin,
He's a Christmas icon.
A bauble, my bauble,
With all the string lights on.

See them, photograph them,
Frame them on your wall.
They are part of nature,
They are part of us all.

An eagle, my eagle,
He rules the land.
A nest, my nest,
He makes a stand.

See them, photograph them,
Frame them on your wall.
They are part of nature,
They are part of us all.

A seagull, my seagull,
They love the sea.

An ice cream, my ice cream
At Brighton beach.

See them, photograph them,
Frame them on your wall.
They are part of nature,
They are part of us all.

Lara Vielvoye (10)
Upper Beeding Primary School, Upper Beeding

Winter

The trees, frozen, as squirrels dance
To the melody of the wind
The fresh water springs
Not flowing but frozen silver.
The cold winter breeze has the voice of an angel.
She calls the flakes of snow to land.

The robin sits perched on a twig
Watching the children play.
He thinks, *how do they play with their winter snow,*
Their hot fire and bountiful winter feast?

But then the last day is here and then...
It stopped. The minutes turned to hours,
Our choirs serenade the church bells.

Ten, nine, eight, seven, six,
Five, four, three, two, one...
We cheer, the new year is here.
We think how lucky we are.

Poppy Johnson (10)
Upper Beeding Primary School, Upper Beeding

Autumn Is Calling

Red leaves on trees are falling,
Silently hitting the ground.
The beginning of autumn is calling,
With a harsh, crisp, whispery sound.

Slowly summer is dying,
It's fading before our eyes.
Far south the birds are flying,
From summer's lonely cries.

Plants and leaves have all faded,
To amber, crimson and brown.
All things living are faded,
No more flowers come out of the ground.

Red leaves on trees have fallen,
They silently hit the ground.
The beginning of autumn is calling,
And summer runs away from the sound.

Nova Redman (10)
Upper Beeding Primary School, Upper Beeding

When The Sun Goes Down

When the sun goes down,
Animals creep out and play,
And make the most of the night,
Predators and prey get into a fight.
Foxes kill rabbits,
And get into weird habits.
I see the red blood,
Making a huge flood.
I can see the dust on the sandy floor,
Whooshing about near the mouse's eyes.
Hyenas let out huge cries,
All the animals save their lives,
The sun is rising in the sky
And for a minute, I wonder why.
The animals come out and play,
But now in their homes they stay.

Layla Antunovich (9)
Upper Beeding Primary School, Upper Beeding

Your Oxygen Supplier

We love trees,
They give us oxygen,
They help us survive,
They help us breathe.

We burn them,
With no care,
There goes another one,
Earning a pound.

You're cutting down your oxygen,
Without a care in the world.
The trees burn and get chopped.

So don't be a fool,
Care about my kind,
Don't kill your oxygen,
For the sake of mankind.

Josh Brian Munns (10)
Upper Beeding Primary School, Upper Beeding

YoungWriters
Est. 1991

YOUNG WRITERS INFORMATION

We hope you have enjoyed reading this book – and that you will continue to in the coming years.

If you're a young writer who enjoys reading and creative writing, or the parent of an enthusiastic poet or story writer, do visit our website **www.youngwriters.co.uk**. Here you will find free competitions, workshops and games, as well as recommended reads, a poetry glossary and our blog.

If you would like to order further copies of this book, or any of our other titles, then please give us a call or visit **www.youngwriters.co.uk**.

Young Writers
Remus House
Coltsfoot Drive
Peterborough
PE2 9BF
(01733) 890066
info@youngwriters.co.uk